HOW CAN I DO ALL THINGS
FOR GOD'S GLORY?

✕ Cultivating Biblical Godliness

Series Editors

Joel R. Beeke and Ryan M. McGraw

Dr. D. Martyn Lloyd-Jones once said that what the church needs to do most of all is "to begin herself to live the Christian life. If she did that, men and women would be crowding into our buildings. They would say, 'What is the secret of this?'" As Christians, one of our greatest needs is for the Spirit of God to cultivate biblical godliness in us in order to put the beauty of Christ on display through us, all to the glory of the triune God. With this goal in mind, this series of booklets treats matters vital to Christian experience at a basic level. Each booklet addresses a specific question in order to inform the mind, warm the affections, and transform the whole person by the Spirit's grace, so that the church may adorn the doctrine of God our Savior in all things.

HOW CAN I DO ALL THINGS
FOR GOD'S GLORY?

JOSEPH A. PIPA JR.

REFORMATION HERITAGE BOOKS
GRAND RAPIDS, MICHIGAN

How Can I Do All Things for God's Glory?
© 2017 by Joseph A. Pipa Jr.

Reformation Heritage Books
2965 Leonard St. NE
Grand Rapids, MI 49525
616-977-0889
orders@heritagebooks.org
www.heritagebooks.org

Printed in the United States of America
17 18 19 20 21 22/10 9 8 7 6 5 4 3 2 1

ISBN 978-1-60178-576-3
ISBN 978-1-60178-577-0 (e-pub)

For additional Reformed literature, request a free book list from Reformation Heritage Books at the above regular or e-mail address.

HOW CAN I DO ALL THINGS
FOR GOD'S GLORY?

B. B. Warfield once told the story of two strangers walking toward each other in a Western town torn by chaos. I will let him relate the story as an officer related it to him:

> One day he observed approaching him a man of singularly combined calmness and firmness of mien, whose very demeanor inspired confidence. So impressed was he with his bearing amid the surrounding uproar that when he had passed he turned to look back at him, only to find that the stranger had done the same. On observing his turning the stranger at once came back to him, and touching his chest with his forefinger, demanded without preface: "What is the chief end of man?" On receiving the countersign, "Man's chief end is to glorify God and to enjoy him forever" — "Ah!" said he, "I knew you were a Shorter Catechism boy by

your looks!" "Why, that was just what I was thinking of you," was the rejoinder.[1]

When Warfield recounts this story, he wants to illustrate that there is a marked piety shaped by the Westminster Shorter Catechism. The foundation for that piety is established in the first question and answer: "What is the chief end of man?"

This concise statement of man's purpose gives meaning and direction to all of life. But I am afraid that this statement, which has become a watchword for Reformed piety, suffers from being treated only as a slogan. We use it so often that we don't think about what we are saying. In particular, what does it mean to glorify God?

GOD'S GLORY

To understand this statement, we must begin with God's glory. We, of course, do not add to God's glory. God's glory is the essence of who He is. As light is essential to the sun, so glory is the essence of God's being. In Acts 7:2, Stephen called Him "the God of glory." His glory is singular, as He claimed in Isaiah 48:11: "I will not give My glory to another."

The essential glory of God is stated succinctly in the Westminster Confession of Faith: "God hath all life, glory, goodness, blessedness, in and of himself;

---

1. Benjamin B. Warfield, *Selected Shorter Writings of Benjamin B. Warfield* (Nutley, N.J.: P&R, 1970), 1:382–83.

and is alone in and unto himself all-sufficient, not standing in need of any creatures which he hath made, not deriving any glory from them, but only manifesting his own glory, in, by, unto, and upon them: he is the alone fountain of all being, of whom, through whom, and to whom, are all things, and hath most sovereign dominion over them, to do by them, for them, or upon them, whatsoever himself pleaseth" (2.2). No mere man can look on this glory, as God said to Moses when he asked to see God's glory: "You cannot see My face; for no man shall see Me, and live" (Ex. 33:20). However, God reveals His glory to us by His names, titles, attributes, ordinances, Word, and works (WSC, Q. 54). When Moses wanted assurance that God would continue in the midst of the people as He promised, he asked God to show him His glory (v. 18). God responded that Moses could not look on His face (His essential glory). Rather, He would place Moses in a cleft of a rock and cause His glory to pass by. He would cover Moses's face while passing and then allow him to see the backside of His glory. But God declared that Moses would learn of His glory from what God said: "I will make all My goodness pass before you, and I will proclaim the name of the LORD before you. I will be gracious to whom I will be gracious, and I will have compassion on whom I will have compassion" (v. 19). Notice that Moses would learn of the glory of God through the proclamation of God's name.

In Exodus 34:6–7, Moses gave an account of what took place: "And the LORD passed before him and proclaimed, 'The LORD, the LORD God, merciful and gracious, long-suffering, and abounding in goodness and truth, keeping mercy for thousands, forgiving iniquity and transgression and sin, by no means clearing the guilty, visiting the iniquity of the fathers upon the children and the children's children to the third and the fourth generation." God revealed His glory in two names: LORD (Jehovah) and God (El). The name "LORD" manifests that God is the eternal, self-sufficient God who makes covenant and redeems His people. The name "God" unfolds His powerful nature as the sovereign, almighty Creator and Governor of all.

Next, God proclaimed five of His attributes: mercy, grace, long-suffering, goodness, and truth. God's attributes are distinguishing characteristics that reveal His glorious nature. The Westminster Shorter Catechism gives an expanded list: "God is a Spirit, infinite, eternal, and unchangeable, in his being, wisdom, power, holiness, justice, goodness, and truth" (Q. 4).

Furthermore, God revealed His glory through His works. He pointed here to His two great works of grace and justice: "keeping mercy for thousands, forgiving iniquity and transgression and sin, by no means clearing the guilty, visiting the iniquity of the fathers upon the children and the children's children to the third and the fourth generation" (v. 7).

Moreover, as the God of glory, He reveals His glory in all His works of creation and providence. In Psalm 148, the psalmist commands us to praise God for His work of creation. He summarizes in verse 13, "Let them praise the name of the LORD, for His name alone is exalted; His glory is above the earth and heaven." In Psalm 104, after detailing God's works of creation, the writer exclaims, "May the glory of the LORD endure forever; may the LORD rejoice in His works" (v. 31). David, in Psalm 29:3, declares of the thunder storm, "The God of glory thunders." God manifests His glory in His works of creation and providence.

But the greatest display of God's glory is in the perfect work of the Lord Jesus Christ, God incarnate. Paul called Him the Lord of glory (1 Cor. 2:8). In heaven, the angels, the living creatures, and the elders shout with a loud voice, "Worthy is the Lamb who was slain to receive power and riches and wisdom, and strength and honor and glory and blessing!" (Rev. 5:12). Hence, if you would see God's glory, you should meditate on His names, titles, attributes, ordinances, Word, and works.

HOW TO GLORIFY GOD

It is here we begin to glorify God. We glorify God as we reflect with love and appreciation on the glory of the Father, Son, and Spirit. In Deuteronomy 6:5, God summons us to love Him: "You shall love the LORD your God with all your heart, with all your soul, and with all your strength." As we commune with the triune God, we are overwhelmed by His beauty and glory. This communion is the beginning of enjoying Him. Some separate enjoying God from glorifying Him. But as we meditate on Him, we begin enjoying Him. We delight in Him. Enjoying God is the privilege of His sons and daughters. It is the abundant life that Christ promises in John 10:10.

This meditation leads to the next act of glorifying God, namely, praising and worshiping Him. So, second, we glorify God when we praise and worship Him. God tells us in Psalm 50:23, "Whoever offers praise glorifies Me." David declared in Psalm 29:1–2: "Give unto the LORD, O you mighty ones, give unto the LORD glory and strength. Give unto the LORD the glory due to His name; worship the LORD in the beauty of holiness."

If we are to glorify God in worship, we must worship Him according to His Word. When God destroyed Nadab and Abihu (Lev. 10:1–2) for not worshiping Him according to His word, He proclaimed, "By those who come near Me I must be regarded as holy; and before all the people I must be glorified" (v. 3). God will only be glorified as we worship Him according to His revealed will. Many theologians refer to this as the regulative principle of worship. The principle is clearly stated in the Westminster Confession of Faith: "But the acceptable way of worshipping the true God is instituted by himself, and so limited by his own revealed will, that he may not be worshipped according to the imaginations and devices of men, or the suggestions of Satan, under any visible representation, or any other way not prescribed in the holy Scripture" (21.1). Some suggest that this was a doctrine peculiar to the Puritans in England, but the Heidelberg Catechism stated the same principle: "What does God require in the second commandment? We are not to make an image of God in any way, nor to worship Him in any other manner than He has commanded in His word" (Q/A 96). And Belgic Confession article 32 expresses the same truth: "We believe that, although it is useful and good for those who govern the Church to establish a certain order to maintain the body of the Church, they must at all times watch that they do not deviate from what Christ, our only Master, has commanded. Therefore, we reject all human inventions and laws introduced into the worship of God which bind and compel the consciences in any way."

One of the principal ways to express God's glory in worship is the use of doxologies. Like the rolling of waves, doxologies pile one ascription of praise upon another. For example, "For of Him and through Him and to Him are all things, to whom be glory forever. Amen" (Rom. 11:36). Or, "Now to the King eternal, immortal, invisible, to God who alone is wise, be honor and glory forever and ever. Amen" (1 Tim. 1:17). Sadly, ascriptions of love and adoration and doxologies are missing in many of our prayers, both public and private. One hundred fifty years ago, William Plumer in his exposition of the third commandment marveled at the neglect of doxologies in public worship: "It is not without cause that some have expressed surprise that doxologies were so little used in social and public worship.... True, we often have them sung at the close of public worship, but they ought to be *said* as well as *sung*."[2] Their spoken use today is relatively rare.

Third, we glorify God when we pray for His name to be hallowed and His kingdom to come (cf. WLC 190–191; WSC 101–102). In Psalm 67:2–3, the psalmist prays, "That Your way may be known on earth, Your salvation among all nations. Let the peoples praise You, O God; let all the peoples praise You." In Psalm 83, where the psalmist prays that God would overthrow the enemies of the church, he concludes, "That they may know that You, whose name alone is the LORD, are the Most High over all the earth" (v. 18). We glorify God as we pray for His glory to be known and His kingdom to come.

Fourth, we glorify God by bearing witness to others of Him, notably of His daily providences and His great redemption. The psalmist called out, "Come and hear, all you who fear God, and I will declare what He has done for my soul" (66:16). Witnessing is simply boasting about God. If He is often in our

---

2. William S. Plumer, *The Law of God as Contained in the Ten Commandments, Explained and Enforced* (Harrisonburg: Sprinkle Publications, 1996), 254.

thoughts, He will be in our speech. This is what Paul taught the Colossians: "Walk in wisdom toward those who are outside, redeeming the time. Let your speech always be with grace, seasoned with salt, that you may know how you ought to answer each one" (Col. 4:5–6). Such speech will provoke people to ask us about what we think and believe: "But sanctify the Lord God in your hearts, and always be ready to give a defense to everyone who asks you a reason for the hope that is in you, with meekness and fear" (1 Peter 3:15).

Fifth, we glorify God when we submit to Him in faith and repentance. When one repents and believes, one is said to glorify God. Luke described the conversion of the Gentiles in Antioch in Pisidia: "Now when the Gentiles heard this, they were glad and glorified the word of the Lord. And as many as had been appointed to eternal life believed" (Acts 13:48). The angel who proclaimed the gospel in Revelation 14:6–7 called out with a loud voice: "Fear God and give glory to Him, for the hour of His judgment has come; and worship Him who made heaven and earth, the sea and springs of water." Joshua used the words, "give glory to the LORD," to express repentance: "Now Joshua said to Achan, 'My son, I beg you, give glory to the LORD God of Israel, and make confession to Him, and tell me now what you have done; do not hide it from me'" (Josh. 7:19). Jeremiah called the people to repentance with the same expression: "Give glory to the LORD your God before He causes darkness, and before your feet stumble on the dark mountains, and while you are looking for light, He turns it into the shadow of death and before He makes it dense darkness" (Jer. 13:16).

Sixth, we glorify God when we believe and honor His word. Isaiah exclaimed, "The LORD is well pleased for His righteousness' sake; He will exalt the law and make it honorable," or, "make it glorious" (42:21). In 1 Timothy 1:11, Paul describes the gospel as "the glorious gospel of the blessed God." Since God reveals His glory in the truth of His Word, we glorify Him when we believe all that He has revealed (WCF 10.2). Part of the proper fear of God is to believe all that He has revealed and to respond to Him according to that revelation. Abraham glorified God by believing the promise: "He did not waver at the promise of God through unbelief, but was strengthened in faith, giving glory to God" (Rom. 4:20). Sinclair Ferguson aptly stated, "The rhythm of the Christian's life is always determined by the principle that when the revelation of God in His glory is grasped by faith, the response is to return all glory to God."[3]

Seventh, we glorify God when we obey Him. Christ teaches us this truth in John 14:15: "If you love Me, keep My commandments." Earlier in the Sermon on the Mount (Matt. 5:16), Jesus stated: "Let your

---

3. Joel R. Beeke, ed., *Living for God's Glory* (Lake Mary, Fla.: Reformation Trust Publishing, 2008), 388.

light so shine before men, that they may see your good works and glorify your Father in heaven." John states, "For this is the love of God, that we keep His commandments. And His commandments are not burdensome" (1 John 5:3).

Christ instructs us in John 15:8: "By this My Father is glorified, that you bear much fruit; so you will be My disciples" (cf. Phil. 1:11). Peter adds, "Having your conduct honorable among the Gentiles, that when they speak against you as evildoers, they may, by your good works which they observe, glorify God in the day of visitation" (1 Peter 2:12).

Eighth, we glorify God as we zealously contend for His honor and truth. When we defend the truth of God's Word, we glorify Him—just as Jude exhorted the recipients of his letter, "Beloved, while I was very diligent to write to you concerning our common salvation, I found it necessary to write to you exhorting you to contend earnestly for the faith which was once for all delivered to the saints" (v. 3). Thomas Watson developed this thought thus: "Much of God's glory lies in his truth. God has intrusted us with his truth, as a master intrusts his servant with his purse to keep. We have not a richer jewel to trust God with than our souls, nor has God a richer jewel to trust us with than his truth. When we are advocates for truth we glorify God."[4]

---

4. Thomas Watson, *The Body of Divinity* (Edinburgh: Banner of Truth, 1974), 15.

Closely related to this is to contend for His honor. When someone we love and respect is insulted, we are indignant and step up to defend that person. When God is dishonored, we should be pierced within. The psalmist cried out, "Zeal for Your house has eaten me up, and the reproaches of those who reproach You have fallen on me (Ps. 69:9; cf. John 2:17). God testified of Phinehas that he turned away God's wrath "because he was zealous with My zeal among them" (Num. 25:11). Watson defined zeal as "a mixed affection, a compound of love and anger; it carries forth our love to God, and our anger against sin in an intense degree. Zeal is impatient of God's dishonor; a Christian fired with zeal, takes a dishonor done to God worse than an injury done to himself."[5]

Ninth, we glorify God when we quietly submit to His will in the difficult circumstances of our lives, confessing with Eli, "It is the LORD. Let Him do what seems good to Him" (1 Sam. 3:18). Job confessed, "Naked I came from my mother's womb, and naked shall I return there. The LORD gave, and the LORD has taken away; blessed be the name of the LORD" (Job 1:21). Not only do we quietly submit, but we also glorify Him as we learn to rejoice in our trials—as James instructs us, "My brethren, count it all joy when you fall into various trials" (James 1:2; cf. Acts 5:41). Thomas Watson explained, "We give God the glory

---

5. Watson, *Body of Divinity*, 16.

of his wisdom, when we rest satisfied with what he carves out to us."[6]

Tenth, we glorify God in the totality of life, in doing all things for His glory. Paul exhorted the church in Corinth in 1 Corinthians 10:31: "Therefore, whether you eat or drink, or whatever you do, do all to the glory of God." Later, he stated: "For you were bought at a price; therefore glorify God in your body and in your spirit, which are God's" (6:20). In all our thoughts, plans, words, and works, we are to seek God's glory. The psalmist summarizes this concept well in Psalm 149:

> Praise the LORD!
> Sing to the LORD a new song,
> And His praise in the assembly of saints.
>
> Let Israel rejoice in their Maker;
> Let the children of Zion be joyful in their King.
> Let them praise His name with the dance;
> Let them sing praises to Him with the timbrel
>   and harp.
> For the LORD takes pleasure in His people;
> He will beautify the humble with salvation.
>
> Let the saints be joyful in glory;
> Let them sing aloud on their beds.
> Let the high praises of God be in their mouth,
> And a two-edged sword in their hand,
> To execute vengeance on the nations,
> And punishments on the peoples;

---

6. Watson, *Body of Divinity*, 13.

To bind their kings with chains,
And their nobles with fetters of iron;
To execute on them the written judgment—
This honor have all His saints.

Praise the LORD!

We are to seek God's glory in all that we do. G. I. Williamson explained, "The true view is that when a person seeks to glorify God, he seeks at all times and in all activities alike to do that which is well pleasing in God's sight. Faithful work, and wholesome recreation, are just as much a part of glorifying God as is the worship of God on the Sabbath, or witnessing to an unbeliever. It is no doubt true that some things that we do are more important than other things. But the true view of Christian discipleship is that which sees the whole of life as that which is to be consciously lived unto the honor of God, and in the service of His name!"[7]

PRINCIPLES FOR GLORIFYING GOD IN ALL THINGS

Well now, how can I glorify God eating a sandwich or mopping a floor? Here is where the difficulty begins. How do I go about a normal day as a business person, housewife, or student, and do all things to the glory of God? I would like to offer six principles which will assist us in doing all things to the

---

7. G. I. Williamson, *The Shorter Catechism, vol. 1: Questions 1–38* (Nutley, N.J.: P&R, 1971), 4.

glory of God. I am sure there are others in the Bible, but these six principles have helped me greatly in this area.

The first principle is that everything must be done according to the commandments of Scripture. Of course, this relates to the seventh point listed above. The commandments of God affect every area of life. All of life's decisions and activities must be in accordance with the revealed will of God. Such a commitment requires a good understanding of the law of God. The place to begin is the exposition of the Ten Commandments as found in the Heidelberg Catechism (Q/A 92–113), the Wesminster Shorter Catechism (Q/A 39–81), and Larger Catechism (Q/A 91–151). To do something to the glory of God, one must do it within the framework of God's law.

One of the purposes of the ceremonial laws in Israel was to train the church in her infancy that God is the Lord of every area of life. Laws, like those governing eating, clothing, farming, and marriage relationships, taught the church in her early years that God governed all of life.

So, I eat to the glory of God by eating in moderation and not overindulging. I do my housework to the glory of God by keeping in mind God's ordained priorities and not putting my house before God and before my family. In my schoolwork, I am careful not to cheat or to allow someone to cheat from my paper. In my vocation, I carefully consider the requirements of the fifth commandment with respect to duties of superiors, equals, and inferiors. To do anything to the glory of God, we must be careful then to examine what we do to see that we are doing it within God's framework.

The second principle is that I am motivated in all I do to please God. What is my motive for doing this thing? Am I doing it to be seen of men or to be seen of God? Paul instructs us in Ephesians 6:5–6: "Bondservants, be obedient to those who are your masters according to the flesh, with fear and trembling, in sincerity of heart, as to Christ; not with eye service, as men-pleasers, but as bondservants of Christ, doing the will of God from the heart." We must do all to please God and not men.

The Christian works hard at his job not to be praised by men or to receive a promotion, but rather because he knows that God is watching and wants him to do his best. The Christian glorifies God in his cultural activity not to be considered the best, but to subdue this part of creation for God's pleasure. So, in order to glorify God, we are to be motivated by His honor and not ours.

The third principle is we glorify God in all of life when we do things to serve our neighbor. The second table of the law is summed up in this way: you are to love your neighbor as yourself. Paul commanded us in Philippians 2:3–4: "Let nothing be done through selfish ambition or conceit, but in lowliness of mind let each esteem others better than himself. Let each of you look out not only for his own interests, but also for the interests of others." The God-glorifying man or woman considers how their actions affect those around them. For example, we drive to the glory of God not only as we respect traffic laws, but as we are considerate of other drivers. We keep our house and yard attractive so as not to detract from our neighbors' yards or property value.

The fourth principle is that we do everything in conscious dependence on God. Romans 11:36 states, "For of Him and through Him and to Him are all things; to whom be glory forever. Amen." We do all things of and through Him. He is the source and means of every task. Paul asserted this principle in Philippians 4:13: "I can do all things through Christ who strengthens me." The Spirit reminds us in Acts 17:28: "For in Him we live and move and have our being."

The Christian is to do nothing in his own strength or ability. Therefore, we pause to give thanks at our meals. We are acknowledging that no matter how wealthy we are, this food is only on our table by the grace of God. The Christian mechanic does not rely only on his own ability, but seeks God's aid in every job. The student prays over his assignments. The Christian housewife seeks the strength and aid of God in all her tasks. The Christian musician seeks the help of God in playing each note. When we depend on God to accomplish our tasks, we are doing them to His glory. Hence, we are to pray about all that we do and act in dependence on the Holy Spirit.

A fifth principle, and closely connected to the fourth, is to give thanks to Him for the things we do. This principle reminds us that we are to do all things and enjoy all things with thankfulness. One of the sins of our age is ingratitude. Think how often Paul included thanksgiving when he exhorted us to pray. For example, Philippians 4:6 directs us: "Be anxious for nothing, but in everything by prayer and supplication, with thanksgiving, let your requests be made known to God." Or Colossians 4:2 states: "Continue earnestly in prayer, being vigilant in it with thanksgiving." The Psalms are full of exhortations to thank God: "Praise the LORD, all you Gentiles! Laud Him, all you peoples! For His merciful kindness is great toward us, and the truth of the LORD endures forever" (Ps. 117:1–2; cf. 100:4; 118:1–4). The sentiment is well expressed in the words of the hymn "Now Thank We All Our God":

> Now thank we all our God
> With heart and hands and voices,
> Who wondrous things hath done,
> In whom His world rejoices;
> Who from our mothers' arms
> Hath blessed us on our way
> With countless gifts of love,
> And still is ours today.

We recognize that all our privileges, benefits, and possessions are tokens of a loving Father. They are pledges to us of our adoption.

We glorify God in all things as we thank Him for them and for the privilege of doing them. We should regularly give thanks, not only for our meals, but also for our possessions, vocations, family, friends, and play. Remember Solomon's counsel: "I know that nothing is better for them than to rejoice, and to do good in their lives, and also that every man should eat and drink and enjoy the good of all his labor—it is the gift of God" (Eccl. 3:12–13).

The sixth principle is that we do all things wholeheartedly. Colossians 3:23 states, "And whatever you do, do it heartily, as to the Lord and not to men." To do something to the glory of God, we put all we have into it; we do not do it halfheartedly.

The Christian works hardest and plays hardest. He doesn't do his work halfheartedly, but gives of his very best; and God is pleased by such effort. The Christian laborer gives a full day's work to his employer. The Christian student gives his full intellectual capacity to his schoolwork.

When we do something to the best of our ability, God will be glorified. He also takes pleasure in us and our activity. In Psalm 149:4, we read: "For the LORD takes pleasure in His people." He not only takes pleasure in our religious exercises, but in all the things in life that we do for His glory. What a joy there is to life when we realize that God is pleased with our work and play. Erik Liddell told his sister in *Chariots of Fire*, "I believe God made me for a purpose, but he also made me fast. And when I run I feel His pleasure."

MOTIVATIONS FOR GLORIFYING GOD

When we think about glorifying God, what are some of the motivations we should consider? First, because He does all things for His glory, we should do all things for His glory also. Everything God has decreed and does is for His glory. Proverbs 16:4 states, "The LORD has made all things for Himself, yes, even the wicked for the day of doom." He is glorified in all His work of creation, but also in His dealing with the wicked. He said of Pharaoh in Exodus 14:17: "And I indeed will harden the hearts of the Egyptians, and they shall follow them. So I will gain honor over Pharaoh and over all his army, his chariots, and his horsemen" (cf. Rom. 9:17). God designed His entire scheme of redemption to bring glory to Himself. Paul spelled out this motivation in Ephesians 1:3–6, teaching that our election and salvation were for His glory—"to the praise of the glory of His grace, by which He made us accepted in the beloved." In 1 Corinthians 1:30–31, Paul demonstrated that all redemption is for God's glory: "But of Him you are in Christ Jesus, who became for us wisdom from God—and righteousness and sanctification and redemption—that, as it is written, 'He who glories, let him glory in the LORD.'" God's glory is His passion; it must be ours.

The second motivation is that we owe Him glory because He is our Maker and Preserver. As Paul argued in Athens, "God, who made the world and everything in it, since He is Lord of heaven and earth, does not dwell in temples made with hands…. And He has made from one blood every nation of men to dwell on all the face of the earth, and has determined their preappointed times and the boundaries of their habitation…for in Him we live and move and have our being" (Acts 17:24, 26, 28). God made us and cares for us. The psalmist proclaims,

> For You have formed my inward parts; You have covered me in my mother's womb. I will praise You, for I am fearfully and wonderfully made; marvelous are Your works, and that my soul knows very well. My frame was not hidden from You, when I was made in secret, and skillfully wrought in the lowest parts of the earth. Your eyes saw my substance, being yet unformed. And in Your book they all were written, the days fashioned for me, when as yet there were none of them. (Ps. 139:13–16)

All people are dependent on God for life and sustenance and are responsible to praise Him. As Christians, aware of this truth, our goal should be to live for His glory.

Third, we are indebted to Him because He has redeemed us, and thus we are to glorify Him in all things. "For you were bought at a price; therefore glorify God in your body and in your spirit, which are God's" (1 Cor. 6:20). We who have been chosen, redeemed, and called belong to God and ought to do all things for His glory. I am greatly indebted to a benefactor who enabled me to study for a doctorate. I love him and would do anything that I could for him and his wife. At times, when my energy flagged in writing the dissertation, I reminded myself of his sacrifice on my behalf. That remembrance served as a great motivation to me to press on. Paul confessed to the sailors that he belonged to God and served Him (Acts 27:23). Matthew Henry, commenting on 1 Corinthians 6:20, wrote: "We must look upon our whole selves as holy to the Lord, and must use our bodies as property which belongs to him and is sacred to his use and service." The Heidelberg Catechism summarized this motivation in Q/A 32: "Since then we are redeemed from our misery by grace through Christ, without any merit of ours, why should we do good works? Because Christ, having redeemed us by His blood, also renews us by His Holy Spirit after His own image, that with our whole life we show ourselves thankful to God for His blessing, and that He be glorified through us."

Fourth, God's glory is the purpose for which we were created and redeemed. God created man in His image so that man would honor God in all things. It is the highest and noblest thing one can do. Isaiah 43:21 states, "This people I have formed for Myself; they shall declare My praise." Peter gave us an apt summary in 1 Peter 2:9: "But you are a chosen generation, a royal priesthood, a holy nation, His own special people, that you may proclaim the praises of Him who called you out of darkness into His marvelous light." God saved us so that we would behold His triune glory in our redemption and that He would be glorified in the redemption of His people.

Fifth, God alone deserves our honor and seeks it. Proverbs 16:4 states, "The LORD has made all for Himself, yes, even the wicked for the day of doom." As we saw above, this thought is expressed in the numerous doxologies of the Bible. One of them is in 1 Timothy 1:17: "Now to the King eternal, immortal, invisible, to God who alone is wise, be honor and glory forever and ever. Amen." Another is later in 1 Timothy: "He who is the blessed and only Potentate, the King of kings and Lord of lords, who alone has immortality, dwelling in unapproachable light, whom no man has seen or can see, to whom be honor and everlasting power. Amen" (6:15–16). Or consider the end of Revelation 5: "Worthy is the Lamb who was slain to receive power and riches and wisdom, and strength and honor and glory and blessing!... Blessing and honor and glory and power be to Him who sits on the throne, and to the Lamb, forever and ever!" (vv. 12–13) We are robbing God of that which is lawfully His by not seeking His glory in everything we think, say, and do.

Sixth, all other creatures exist for God's glory and bring glory to Him. Everything in the inanimate creation glorifies God by its very existence and activity. "The heavens declare the glory of God; and the firmament shows His handiwork" (Ps. 19:1). Similarly, the animate creatures glorify Him, as Isaiah exclaimed: "The beast of the field will honor Me, the jackals and the ostriches" (43:20). The same is true of all heavenly beings. Commenting on the role of the angels in Hebrews 1:14, Thomas Watson wrote: "They are still waiting on God's throne, and bring some revenues of glory into the exchequer of heaven. Surely man should be much more studious of God's glory than the angels; for God has honoured him more than the angels, in that Christ took man's nature upon him, and not the angels.'"[8] Since all creatures exist for God's glory, how much more should we, who are being renewed in His image, labor for His glory.

Seventh, seeking God's glory in all of life brings the greatest enjoyment of life. We began with the answer of the Westminster Shorter Catechism which instructs us that man's chief end is to glorify God and to enjoy Him forever. The enjoyment of God is the end result of our glorifying Him. As we glorify God in life, we will enjoy God. As we enjoy God, all of life becomes sacred service. The enjoyment of God is the greatest good in this life and in the life to come. Learn from Asaph: "Whom have I in heaven but You? And there is none upon earth that I desire

8. Watson, *Body of Divinity*, 10.

besides You. My flesh and my heart fail; but God is the strength of my heart and my portion forever" (Ps. 73:25–26).

When life's props fail, none will be able to take away our greatest pleasure, as Habakkuk 3:17–18 testified:

> Though the fig tree may not blossom,
> Nor fruit be on the vines;
> Though the labor of the olive may fail,
> And the fields yield no food;
> Though the flock may be cut off from the fold,
> And there be no herd in the stalls—
> Yet I will rejoice in the LORD,
> I will joy in the God of my salvation.

When we seek to glorify God in all things, our joy will be full, and none will be able to take it away from us.